The 1001-Day Amazing Air Fryer Cookbook UK

Quick and Healthy Recipes That Will Improve
Your Kitchen Game incl. Sides & More

John R. Sinclair

ISBN - 9798354820528

TABLE OF CONTENTS

EXCLUSIVE BONUS

40 Weight Loss Recipes

&

14 Days Meal Plan

Scan the QR-Code and receive
the FREE download:

Introduction

Every now and then, most people want a quick and delicious fried meal. The problem is that along with that delicious goodness, comes a lot of negative effects on your health, both in the moment, as well as down the road. So what do you do when you want those fried foods, but you also want to stay healthy?

There is one appliance available that can give you that crispy yummy food and still allow you to stay on the straight and narrow when it comes to your health. What appliance can do that? An air fryer! Not only will you be able to keep healthy, but you will also be able to have scrumptious meals quickly with little preparation.

If you're wondering what type of meals to make in your air fryer, make sure to check out the wide variety of recipes in this cookbook.

What is an Air Fryer?

When you hear the words air fryer, you may immediately focus on the word fryer. This appliance is in no way related to the deep fryer used to create many of the meals below traditionally. In fact, the air fryer couldn't be more different from that appliance. Air fryers are pieces of equipment that cook food with a fan that creates high temperatures.

Unlike a fryer, the air fryer uses reduced levels of oil and sometimes no oil at all. The system of an air fryer also requires no time for pre-heating like a traditional oven or deep fryer. The build of the fryer also offers even cooking. Now that you have an idea of what an air fryer is and how it works, let's look at how you use one.

How To Use It

So the best use of this appliance is to give you more versatility in meal choices that are healthy and delicious. The food requires, as we said, little to no oil to crisp up and that inherently leads to more healthy meals.

Air fryers can be used for a lot of different things. They work well with frozen or raw foods. With the meat, they will not require a lot of oil to get crispy and yet will still stay juicy as well. In regards to meat, the leaner cuts will require a little more oil.

Such meats like chicken or pork will need a little spritz of oil. The best option will be a vegetable-based oil. Vegetables, too, will need to be coated with oil and seasoning before using the air fryer.

Air Fryer Maintenance

So air fryers are fantastic, as you can see, but even though they are easy to use, they still require a little upkeep and maintenance. If you want your air fryer to last longer, maintaining a proper schedule for cleaning and maintenance will help extend the life of this appliance.

How to Clean Your Air Fryer

So the first part of the maintenance and upkeep of the air fryer is the clean up after use. Though each model may come with different tools and suggestions for cleaning, there is a standard practice that can be used across the board.

Here are the steps:

- The first step is to unplug the air fryer and make sure that the unit, if recently used, is cooled completely.

- Then wet a washcloth and wipe down the outside of the unit.

- Now you will want to remove the tray and any accessories that you used. Then taking hot water with some dish soap, use a sponge or rag to wash them. Then take them and place them in the dishwasher.

- Once all the accessories have been removed from the unit, you can take the damp washcloth and wipe down the inside of the air fryer as well.

- You will want to ensure that you get all the food removed from the heating element. You may need to use a brush to do this.

- When the dishwasher is done, remove the tray and accessories and let them completely dry. When they are, you can replace them in the unit.

Storing Your Air Fryer

Storing an appliance is often overlooked in the maintenance process, but it plays a vital role as well. When you store it, you will want to make sure it has fully cooled down. Then when you go to put it in the cabinet, make sure you store it right side up. You will also want to role the cord into the storage compartment or wrapped neatly behind the unit.

Maintenance of Your Air Fryer

So other than keeping the unit properly cleaned, there are also some standard maintenance tasks that you should incorporate into your routine.

Here are some of those:

- Make sure to check the cords every time you use the fryer. By doing this, you will be able to tell if the plug and wire have been damaged or have begun to fray. Knowing this before you plug it in can prevent accidents and serious injuries. Also, in regards to the cord, like the unit itself, you will want to make sure that it is clean before using the unit.

- Cleanliness is also, as we said, a part of the maintenance and upkeep. That means if you haven't used the fryer in a while, you may want to do a quick cleaning. This can remove any debris that you missed or get rid of any dust and particles that have collected when the unit has been out of service.

- Next up is a look at the distance between the unit and the wall socket or other appliances on the kitchen cabinet. The unit, to work properly, needs about four inches behind and above the unit work properly. This gives the unit enough room to get rid of the steam and heat while it cooks. If you place the unit in a place where they don't have enough space, the units can overheat.

- When getting ready to use your unit, you will want to make sure that it is situated on a flat surface.

- Like the cord, you should also take a good look at the individual components and accessories. Inspect these pieces to detect if there are any damages or issues that may be a problem.

Potential Issues & Resolutions

- Smell that won't go away – Sometimes, when you cook food that has a strong odor, you may find that it stays around long after the meal is completed. In order to get rid of that smell, you will want to make sure that your clean the fryer after every use. If the smell still is present after cleaning the unit, then you may want to soak the accessories and pans in hot water and soap for an hour or so. Another way to remove the odor is to cut a lemon in half and rub the accessories and pan down.

- Peeling or bubbling up of coating – Typically, air fryers are coated with non-stick coating. If it gets scratched, sometimes, when used, you will start to see the coating bubble. If it's on the outside, it is not really something to concern you. If, on the other hand, it is on the interior of the unit, you may want to see if your unit is covered by the warranty.

- ■ White smoke – Typically, this happens when there is too much grease from the meal. When this grease gathers, the heat will cause it to break down. This can cause excessive smoke. The smoke won't affect the food but can be very annoying. The best way to overcome this is to make sure everything is clean. You should also manage the grease while cooking the meal too.

Tips & Tricks, Etc.

So whenever you get a new piece of equipment or appliance in your kitchen, you want to be able to get the most from it. After all, you invested your hard-earned money, and you want to ensure it was spent on something that will return that investment. That means understanding how to choose the best one for your needs as well as how to really get the biggest bang for your buck.

With that being said, we have pulled together a few things that you should look for when choosing your air fryer. Along with that, we have also compiled an awesome list of tips and tricks that will help you use the air fryer you chose to its fullest.

Let's start with what to look for.

What to Look For When Buying

There are a lot of factors that can be used as the measuring stick of what is the right choice for you when it comes to an air fryer. Among these factors are:

Capacity

Air fryers most often come in one of two sizes – 2 and 7 quarts. You will want to consider that when looking for the right fryer. This can be important in two different ways. The first is going to be in regards to the space you have. A larger capacity fryer will take up more space. This means if you don't have a lot of room to play with, you may have to go with the smaller option.

Along with the space you have, you should also consider the number of people you will be looking to feed with this air fryer. If you have a small family, you may still be able to go with the smaller unit. However, if you have a large family, you will have to opt for the larger air fryer.

Presets

Another factor to look at is the presets that come built into the unit. Each model will come with its own presets. Some will have two or three others that may have upwards of 11. Each one will help you make your meal preparation easier and faster than going the traditional route.

Additional Features

When looking at an air fryer, if you're dealing with limited space, you may want to choose an air fryer that does double duty. Some air fryers come with these additional features:

- **Toaster Oven** – This may be the most common extra feature. This style of air fryer looks very similar to the toaster oven and has all the capabilities of that appliance plus the air fryer.

- **Dehydrator** - If you like to make trail mixes or preserve foods, a dehydrator may be a nice additional feature.

- **Rotisserie** – If you love moist chickens, then finding an air fryer that also has a rotisserie feature included.

Price

The last factor we would suggest paying attention to is the price tag. This is especially important if you are dealing with a tight budget. You want to get the most for the money you spend. Air fryers have a wide range of price tags. You just have to find the one that matches your needs.

Tips & Tricks

Before we get into the recipes, let's talk about some tips you can use to make the unit work harder for you and to maximize the flavors of the meal. Here are some key tips to keep in mind when using an air fryer:

- **Preheat the air fryer** – there are, of course, some meals that don't have to have the unit pre-heated, but for the most part, you should not skip this step. Like with an oven pre-heating will allow a faster and more oven cook of the food.

- **Spray the basket with cooking spray** – though the air fryer is designed with a non-stick coating, you will still want to add a little spray or oil to make sure that food does not stick. You will want to stay away from high smoking oils like soybean. You should stick with vegetable-based oils like olive or avocado.

- **Add water to the fryer drawer when cooking fatty foods** – Things like bacon can be cooked in the air fryer. When it cooks, it releases a ton of grease and fat if there is nothing to catch it, and this could cause a bit of smoke. You could drain the tray if you wanted, but a better option would be to place a little water in the bottom.

- **Capture the grease and use it to make sauces** – The fat from the meals you cook is captured in the drip tray. This, like the fat rendered in a skillet, can be used to make gravies later. So drain it and place it in some storage container for another day.

- **Shake the basket** – if you want an even cook, you should definitely remember to shake the basket or tray a few times during the cooking cycle. This is really important for small things like tater tots or fries to make sure that everything gets nice and crisp.

- **Don't overcrowd the fryer** – The air fryer cooks by moving heated air through the compartment. This means if there is too much in that compartment, it will hinder the consistency of the airflow. This will lead to uneven cooking and longer cooking times. It is better to cook in batches to ensure crisp well-cooked meals.

- **Cook in a single even layer** – If you are cooking thicker foods like pork chops or steak, you will want to make sure that you place them in the tray in a single layer. Stacking them will cause a lack of color and crispness. If you have to cook more than what fits in the tray, you will have to cook in batches to ensure a proper cook.

- **Line tray with parchment/foil** – If you don't want to have a lengthy cleanup process when you are done, then you may want to line the tray. You can line it with aluminum foil or even parchment paper. This is really only a good idea with heavier foods. Lighter foods may allow the foil or paper to move around due to the circulation of air.

- **Use the fryer to toast nuts** – If you want to toast some nuts don't bother pre-heating the oven. Instead, use your air fryer. The use of heated circulated air to cook allows for good toasting. All you have to do is toss the nuts with whatever seasoning you like and craft yourself a nice afternoon snack.

- **Mix seasoning into the oil** – Spices that are lighter in weight may be blown around in the fryer if not glued down. So how do you glue your seasoning to the food you are cooking? The best way is to mix it in with an oil and lightly baste the food with it. This will ensure that the seasonings stay in place and work their way into the meal you are preparing.

- **Don't use aerosol sprays** – There are non-stick cooking sprays that are crafted with things that can damage the coating your air fryer is built with. So you want to stay away from those. Instead, try to use a spray bottle and your chosen oil for your cooking needs.

- **Spray food halfway through cooking** – Another great tip when using a fryer helps you achieve a super crispy finish. Halfway through the cooking process, you should remove the tray and hit the meal with a light spraying of oil.

- **Buy a good thermometer** – One great addition to your air frying kit might be a good quick-read thermometer. This will help you achieve a proper temperature when dealing with meats. Every meat has a perfect internal temp, and when cooking in an air fryer, it is not easy to read that quickly. You want a quick read so that you don't allow too much-heated air to escape. This will make sure that your meat is always entirely cooked so that you don't have to fear getting sick.

- **Reheating Food** – You can use the air fryer to reheat leftovers too. You will have to play it by ear to find the right temp for the perfect reheating. A good temp to start with is 350°F.

- **Tie food down** – If you are cooking lighter foods, then you may want to keep them in place. In order to do that, you can use toothpicks to keep stacked foods together. This can be useful when using the air fryer to make a sandwich or a quesadilla.

- **Place the fryer under the stove hood** – There will be some steam and/or smoke. So placing the unit under the hood of your stove will allow you to keep the air free of smoke or steam.

EXCLUSIVE BONUS

40 Weight Loss Recipes

&

14 Days Meal Plan

Scan the QR-Code and receive
the FREE download:

Breakfast

Walnut & Cinnamon Baked Apples

SERVINGS: 2

INGREDIENTS:

- 1 med. apple
- 2 tbsps. pecans, chopped
- 2 tbsps. raisins
- 1½ tsps. butter
- ¼ tsp. cinnamon
- ¼ tsp. nutmeg
- ¼ cup/ 59ml water

DIRECTIONS:

1. Preheat the air fryer to 350°F/ 177˚C. Cut the apple in half and hollow out the center leaving a little wall.

2. Place the apple on the air fryer pan. In a small mixing bowl, combine everything else but the water. Divide mixture between apples.

3. In a little bowl, join margarine, cinnamon, nutmeg, pecans, and raisins.

4. Spoon this blend into the focuses of the apple/pear parts.

5. Empty water into the pan and cook for about 20 minutes.

NUTRITIONAL FACTS:
CALORIES: 115
PROTEINS: 2.2G
CARBS: 15.3G
FATS: 6.2G

Cheesy Sausage & Pepper Breakfast Casserole

SERVINGS: 8

INGREDIENTS:

- 1 lb. / 454g pork sausage, ground
- ¼ cup / 57g onion, diced
- 1 bell pepper, green, diced
- 8 eggs
- ½ cup / 113g Colby jack cheese, shredded
- 1 tsp. fennel seed
- ½ tsp. garlic salt

DIRECTIONS:

1. In a medium-sized skillet brown the sausage. Then add the peppers and let cook for a few minutes longer. While it is browning, in a small bowl, beat the eggs until combined.

2. After spraying the air fryer dish with cooking spray, place the sausage mix into the base and cover with cheese. Then pour over the egg mixture. Then take the Air Fryer dish and shower it with non-stick cooking splash.

3. Then top the casserole with seasonings and place in the air fryer. Cook for 15 minutes on 390˚F / 199˚C. Remove and let sit for a minute. Then cut and serve.

NUTRITIONAL FACTS:
CALORIES: 282
PROTEINS: 15G
CARBS: 3G
FATS: 23G

Cinnamon Rolls

SERVINGS: 8

INGREDIENTS:

- 1 lb. / 454g frozen bread dough, defrosted
- ¼ cup / 57g butter
- ¾ cup/ 57g brown sugar
- 1½ tbsps. ground cinnamon

Glaze

- 4 oz. / 113g cream cheese
- 2 tbsps. butter
- 1¼ cups / 284g powdered sugar
- ½ tsp. vanilla extract

DIRECTIONS:

1. Let the bread mixture come to room temperature. Flour the working surface and roll out mix into a rectangle, making sure that the longest side is toward you. Brush melted butter over the top of the dough but leave a 1" / 2.5cm border butterless.

2. In a mixing bowl, combine the sugar and cinnamon. When combined, sprinkle the mixture evenly over dough, maintaining the border. Fold into a log beginning with the edge nearest to you. Tightly roll the log and push out any air pockets. When you reach the edge of the batter, press the edges of the dough to seal it together.

3. Cut into 8 pieces. Lay slices onto a kitchen towel and let rise for 1½ to 2 hours. When the rolls have risen, pre-heat the air fryer to 350ºF / 177ºC. Place four of the rolls in the air fryer and cook for 5 minutes and then turn them over and cook for another 4 minutes. Repeat with remaining rolls.

4. While the rolls are cooking, combine the cream cheese and butter. Then microwave for 30 seconds. Once softened, then begin to slowly incorporate the powdered sugar and vanilla. Set to the side.

5. Let the cinnamon rolls cool for a few minutes before glazing them. Serve warm!

NUTRITIONAL FACTS:
CALORIES: 424
PROTEINS: 4G
CARBS: 67G
FATS: 15G

Sugared Doughnuts

SERVINGS: 8

INGREDIENTS:

- 2 packages premade croissant dough
- ½ cup / 113g sugar
- 2 tsps. ground cinnamon
- 4 tbsps. butter
- coconut oil cooking spray

DIRECTIONS:

1. Mix the sugar and cinnamon together in a bowl; set aside.

2. Remove rolls from the package and separate laying them on a flat working surface. Using a cookie cutter make doughnut shapes.

3. Lightly spray the air fryer rack with cooking spray and place four of the doughnuts on it. Make sure they are not touching.

4. Bake at 360ºF / 182ºC for 5 minutes. Remove from the fryer and brush with melted butter. Then toss with cinnamon/sugar blend.

NUTRITIONAL FACTS:
CALORIES: 316
PROTEINS: 3G
CARBS: 42G
FATS: 15G

Cranberry Nut Muffins

SERVINGS: 8

INGREDIENTS:

- ¼ cup / 59ml cashew milk
- 2 lrg. eggs
- ½ tsp. vanilla extract
- ½ cups / 113g almond flour
- ¼ cup / 57g Monkfruit
- 1 tsp. baking powder
- ¼ tsp. cinnamon
- 1/8 tsp. salt
- ½ cup / 113g cranberries, fresh
- ¼ cup / 57g walnuts, chopped

DIRECTIONS:

1. In a mixer, combine the milk, eggs, and vanilla extract. Mix until combined. Then add in the flour, sugar, baking powder, cinnamon, and salt – mix another 30-45 seconds until thoroughly combined.

2. Remove the mixing bowl and then fold in the cranberries and nuts. Spoon the mixture into silicone muffin tin.

3. Place in the fryer and bake at 325ºF / 163ºC for 12-15 minutes. Remove from the fryer and let cool on a rack.

NUTRITIONAL FACTS:
CALORIES: 51
PROTEINS: 1.3G
CARBS: 3.2G
FATS: 3.7G

Avocado Cups

SERVINGS: 4

INGREDIENTS:

- 2 avocados, halved
- 2 tomatoes, diced
- ¼ cup / 57g diced red onion
- 2 tbsps. cilantro, fresh, chopped
- 1 tbsp. jalapeno, diced fine
- 1 tbsp. lime juice
- ½ tsp. salt
- ¼ tsp. pepper
- 4 eggs

DIRECTIONS:

1. Halve the avocados and scoop out the inside. Then dice the avocado and in a small bowl, combine it with the tomato, onion, cilantro, jalapeno, juice, salt, and pepper. Cover and refrigerate until ready to use.

2. Preheat the air fryer to 350ºF / 177ºC. To guarantee that avocado shells don't move while cooking, place a foil ring around each one.

3. Set every avocado shell in a foil ring on the air fryer sheet. Break 1 egg into every avocado shell and air-fry 5 to 7 minutes. Remove and serve topped with avocado salsa.

NUTRITIONAL FACTS:
CALORIES: 240
PROTEINS: 4.9G
CARBS: 15.7G
FATS: 19.3G

French Toast Sticks

SERVINGS: 2

INGREDIENTS:

- 4 pcs. bread
- 2 tbsp butter
- 2 eggs
- 1 pinch of salt
- 1 pinch of cinnamon
- 1 pinch of nutmeg
- 1 pinch of ground cloves
- 1 tsp. powdered sugar

DIRECTIONS:

1. Preheat the air fryer to 356ºF / 180ºC. In a bowl, beat together the eggs, a sprinkle of salt, cinnamon, nutmeg, and ground cloves.

2. Butter the two sides of the bread and cut into strips. Dip each strip in the egg blend and place them on the air fryer sheet.

3. After 2 minutes in the fryer, remove the strips and coat lightly with cooking spray on both sides. Return to the fryer and cook for another 4 minutes.

4. When the egg is cooked, and bread is browned, remove and serve topped with powdered sugar and warmed maple syrup for dunking.

NUTRITIONAL FACTS:
CALORIES: 178
PROTEINS: 5G
CARBS: 2G
FATS: 15G

Keto Style Baked Eggs

SERVINGS: 1

INGREDIENTS:

- 1 lrg. egg
- 1 tbsp. milk
- 1 tbsp. spinach, fresh, sautéed
- 2 tsps. cheddar, shredded
- Salt and pepper to taste
- Cooking spray

DIRECTIONS:

1. Lightly spray a ramekin with cooking spray of your choice. Then add in the spinach and crack an egg over it. Top the egg with cheese and season to taste with salt and pepper. Gently mix the ingredients together, being careful not to puncture the yolk.

2. Air fry at 330°F / 166°C for approximately 6. Remove and serve with your favorite breakfast sides.

NUTRITIONAL FACTS:
CALORIES: 115
PROTEINS: 10G
CARBS: 1G
FATS: 7G

Vegetable Quiche

SERVINGS: 2

INGREDIENTS:

- 1 head broccoli
- 3 lrg. carrots
- 1 lrg. tomato
- 3.5 oz. / 100g cheddar, grated
- 1 oz. / 20g feta

- 5 oz. / 150ml milk
- 2 lrg. eggs
- 1 tsp. parsley
- 1 tsp. thyme
- Salt and pepper to taste

DIRECTIONS:

1. Cut the broccoli into florets and then prepare the rest of the vegetables. Place broccoli and carrots on a fryer sheet and cook until tender. Then place in an air fryer safe quiche dish.

2. Add all the seasonings and crack the eggs into the bowl. Whisk until combined. Then begin adding the milk until the mixture is pale.

3. Then layer the tomatoes and top with cheese. Pour the egg mixture over the mix in the quiche dish and top with remaining cheese. Place in the fryer and cook for 20 minutes on 356°F / 180°C. Serve.

```
NUTRITIONAL FACTS:
CALORIES: 488
PROTEINS: 31G
CARBS: 36G
FATS: 26G
```

Chorizo & Egg Burritos

SERVINGS: 8

INGREDIENTS:

- ◆ 1 lb. / 454g breakfast sausage
- ◆ 1 bell pepper, sliced
- ◆ 12 eggs
- ◆ ½ tsp. pepper
- ◆ 1 tsp. salt
- ◆ 8 flour tortillas
- ◆ 2 cups / 510g cheddar, shredded

DIRECTIONS:

1. In a skillet brown the sausage. Then when browned, add in the peppers and sauté for a few minutes. Remove sausage and peppers and let drain on a paper towel. Set to the side.

2. In the same skillet, soften the butter and add in the eggs, salt, and pepper, and cook over medium heat, mixing consistently, until the eggs are cooked. Once that is done, lay out the tortillas. Spoon a small bit of sausage and pepper mix into the center of each tortilla. Top this with the egg mix and sprinkle cheese on top. Roll each burrito.

3. Preheat the air fryer to 390°F / 199°C. Spray the burrito lightly with cooking spray.

4. Place burritos in the air fryer and cook for 3 minutes at 390°F / 199°C. Repeat until all burritos are browned.

5. Remove and cook immediately with your favorite toppings.

NUTRITIONAL FACTS:
CALORIES: 283
PROTEINS: 16G
CARBS: 16G
FATS: 17G

Lunch

Avocado Fries W/ Bacon

SERVINGS: 4

INGREDIENTS:

- 3 avocados
- 24 slices bacon

- ¼ cup / 59ml ranch, for serving

DIRECTIONS:

1. Cut every avocado into 8 wedges. Wrap each wedge with a portion of bacon, cutting the bacon if necessary.

2. In batches, place in the air fryer and cook at 400°F / 204°C for 8 minutes until bacon is cooked through and firm.

3. Serve warm with ranch dressing for dipping.

NUTRITIONAL FACTS:
CALORIES: 120
PROTEINS: 4G
CARBS: 3G
FATS: 2G

Antipasto Pockets

SERVINGS: 12

INGREDIENTS:

- 12 egg roll wrappers
- 12 slices provolone
- 12 slices deli ham
- 36 slices pepperoni
- 1 cup / 227g mozzarella, shredded
- 1 cup / 227g pepperoncini, sliced
- Vegetable oil
- ¼ cup / 57g Parmesan, grated
- Italian dressing

DIRECTIONS:

1. Place one wrapper down and add a slice of provolone in the middle. Layer on the ham, pepperoni, and add on the mozzarella and pepperoncini's. Then roll and wrap like an egg roll. Seal the pocket with a little water.

2. Working in batches, cook the pockets at 390°F / 199°C until browned, around 12 minutes, flipping part of the way through. Then serve warm or cooled with Italian dressing for dipping.

NUTRITIONAL FACTS:
CALORIES: 284
PROTEINS: 22.1G
CARBS: 20.6G
FATS: 12.2G

Chicken Stuffed Quesadilla

SERVINGS: 4

INGREDIENTS:

- 2 corn tortillas
- 3 tbsps. premade guacamole
- 1/3 cup / 85g cheddar ground
- ½ cup / 100g chicken breast, shredded

DIRECTIONS:

1. Preheat air fryer to 325°F /170°C. Lightly spray the air fryer basket with cooking spray. Set the bottom tortilla inside the air fryer. Then evenly spread on the guacamole and cheddar. Top this with chicken and top with the second tortilla.

2. Use a toothpick to fasten the top tortilla while cooking. Cook for 6-10 minutes, cautiously flipping the quesadilla over part of the way through. Once cooked to your liking, remove, cut, and serve with your favorite quesadilla garnishes and dipping sauces.

NUTRITIONAL FACTS:
CALORIES: 106
PROTEINS: 7G
CARBS: 7G
FATS: 6G

Cauliflower Bites

SERVINGS: 6

INGREDIENTS:

- Cooking spray
- 4 cups / 907g cauliflower florets
- 1 lrg. egg
- 1 cup / 227g cheddar, shredded
- 1 cup / 227g Parmesan, grated
- 2/3 cup / 70g panko breadcrumbs
- 2 tbsps. chives, fresh, chopped
- Salt and pepper to taste
- ½ cup / 118ml ketchup
- 2 tbsps. Sriracha

DIRECTIONS:

3. Steam the cauliflower, and when tender, add to a food processor. Pulse until rice and then lay the riced cauliflower out on a towel. Press to remove as much water as possible.

4. Add cauliflower into a large mixing bowl along with egg, cheddar, parmesan, breadcrumbs, and chives. Mix gently until thoroughly combined and season with salt and pepper to taste.

5. Spoon a small portion out and form into a tater tot shape. Working in groups, lay the tots out in an even layer on the air fryer sheet and cook at 375°F / 191°C for 10, until browned.

6. While the bites are cooking, combine the ketchup and sriracha in a mixing bowl and stir to combine. Serve warm cauliflower bites with spicy ketchup.

NUTRITIONAL FACTS:
CALORIES: 187
PROTEINS: 12.5G
CARBS: 14.6G
FATS: 9.1G

Crispy Chicken Fingers

SERVINGS: 4

INGREDIENTS:

Chicken Fingers

- ½ lb. / 227g chicken strips
- Salt and pepper to taste
- ½ cup / 113g all-purpose flour
- 2½ cup / 266g panko bread pieces
- 2 lrg. eggs
- ¼ cup / 59ml buttermilk
- Cooking splash

Honey Mustard

- 1/3 cup / 78ml mayonnaise
- 3 tbsps. honey
- 2 tbsps. Dijon mustard
- ¼ tsp. hot sauce
- Salt and pepper to taste

DIRECTIONS:

1. Season chicken with salt and pepper. Set up a dredging station with a bowl for each the flour, breadcrumbs and beaten eggs and buttermilk mixture. Dip chicken in flour, then the egg mixture and then into breadcrumbs. Let the chicken sit for a few minutes and then begin cooking in batches.

2. Place chicken in the air fryer, being sure not to overcrowd. Lightly spray the tops of the chicken with cooking spray and cook at 400°F / 204°C for 5 minutes. Flip chicken over, spray this side with more oil and cook 5 minutes more. Repeat for all the chicken fingers.

3. While cooking the chicken fingers, add all the ingredients for the honey mustard into a mixing bowl. Season to taste with salt and pepper and stir to combine. Serve chicken fingers warm with dipping sauce.

NUTRITIONAL FACTS:
CALORIES: 568
PROTEINS: 44.7G
CARBS: 61.7G
FATS: 14.7G

Thai-Style Salmon Cakes

SERVINGS: 7

INGREDIENTS:

- 14 oz. / 400 g canned salmon
- ½ cup / 53g Panko breadcrumbs
- ¼ tsp. salt
- ½ tbsp. red curry paste
- ½ tbsp. brown sugar
- 1 lime, zested
- 2 eggs
- Cooking spray

DIRECTIONS:

1. Combine all ingredients until they are all combined thoroughly, and the salmon is evenly distributed throughout the mix. Form mixture into patties.

2. Heat the air fryer to 360°F / 180°C. Spray patties with oil on both sides lightly.

3. Place patties into the fryer. Cook for 4 minutes, flip, and cook for 4 additional minutes.

4. Move to a plate and repeat with remaining patties. Serve with a nice salad or as a salmon burger.

NUTRITIONAL FACTS:
CALORIES: 108
PROTEINS: 12G
CARBS: 6G
FATS: 6G

Sweet Potato Fries

SERVINGS: 2

INGREDIENTS:

- 2 med. sweet potatoes, cut into sticks
- 1 tbsp. olive oil, extra-virgin
- ½ tsp. garlic powder
- ½ tsp chili powder
- Salt and pepper to taste

Dipping Sauce

- 2 tbsps. mayonnaise
- 2 tbsps. barbeque sauce
- 1 tsp. hot sauce

DIRECTIONS:

1. In a bowl, toss the sweet potatoes with the seasonings and oil. Then season to taste with salt and pepper.

2. In batches, place fries in the fryer basket and cook at 375°F / 191°C for 8 minutes, flip fries, and cook 8 minutes more.

3. While cooking the fries make the dipping sauce. Add all the ingredients into a mixing bowl and stir until combined. Then serve with warm fries.

> NUTRITIONAL FACTS:
> CALORIES: 225
> PROTEINS: 3.4G
> CARBS: 35.3G
> FATS: 8.2G

Tofu Bits

SERVINGS: 4

INGREDIENTS:

- 12 oz. / 350 g extra firm tofu
- 1 tbsp. avocado oil
- 2 tsps. cornstarch
- 1 tsp. paprika
- 1 tsp. onion powder
- 1 tsp. garlic powder
- ½ tsp. pepper
- ½ tsp. salt

DIRECTIONS:

1. Start by pressing the tofu to remove excess water. Sandwich the block between paper towels and two plates. Then place a heavier item on top and let press for about half an hour.

2. Heat air fryer to 390°F / 199°C. Cut tofu into cubes. Toss the cubes in the oil and then the cornstarch.

3. Coat the tofu with remaining ingredients and place in the fryer. Cook for 13 minutes, shaking at regular intervals.

4. Serve warm with a dipping sauce of your choice.

NUTRITIONAL FACTS:
CALORIES: 94
PROTEINS: 6G
CARBS: 5G
FATS: 5G

Crunchy Cheese Sticks

SERVINGS: 2

INGREDIENTS:

- 6 mozzarella sticks
- 1 cup / 107g panko breadcrumbs
- Salt and pepper to taste
- 2 lrg. eggs
- 3 tbsps. all-purpose flour
- Warm marinara for dipping

DIRECTIONS:

1. Freeze mozzarella sticks until cold. Then set up a breading station: Place panko, eggs, and flour in three separate dishes. Season panko with salt and pepper.

2. Coat mozzarella sticks in flour, then in egg, followed by the point panko, back into the egg, and finally one more time into the panko.

3. Spread mozzarella sticks in an even layer in the air fryer. Cook on 400°F / 204°C for 6 minutes, or until the coating is crispy and brown.

4. Serve with warm marinara sauce to dip the sticks in.

NUTRITIONAL FACTS:
CALORIES: 144
PROTEINS: 5.5G
CARBS: 18.2G
FATS: 5.2G

Pizza Margherita

SERVINGS: 2

INGREDIENTS:

- 2 bundles pizza dough
- 1 tbsp. olive oil. extra-virgin
- 1/3 cup / 78ml crushed tomatoes
- 1 clove garlic, minced
- ½ tsp. oregano
- Salt and pepper to taste
- ½ mozzarella ball, sliced
- Basil leaves

DIRECTIONS:

1. On a floured surface, stretch the pizza dough out. Then brush with olive oil and place the oil side up into the air fryer.

2. In a bowl, mix the tomatoes, garlic, and oregano. Spoon half the mixture into the center of the dough and spread evenly over the surface. Make sure to leave an edge around the entire pizza unsauced.

3. Add a large portion of the mozzarella slices to the pizza. Air fry on 400°F / 204°C for 10 to 12 minutes, or until the crust is lightly browned and the cheese melted.

4. Remove the first pizza from the air fryer and garnish with basil. Repeat the process with the second pizza.

> NUTRITIONAL FACTS:
> CALORIES: 724
> PROTEINS: 26.3G
> CARBS: 70.8G
> FATS: 37.7G

Dinner

Asian Glazed Chicken

SERVINGS: 4

INGREDIENTS:

- 8 chicken thighs, boneless, skinless
- ¼ cup / 59ml soy sauce
- 2½ tbsps. balsamic vinegar
- 1 tbsp. honey
- 3 cloves garlic, minced
- 1 tsp. Sriracha
- 1 tsp. ginger, fresh, grated
- 1 scallion, chopped

DIRECTIONS:

1. In a bowl, combine the honey, soy sauce, balsamic, sriracha, garlic, and ginger. Mix until thoroughly combined.

2. Pour half of the mixture into a bowl with the chicken, covering all the meat and let sit in the refrigerator for 2 hours. Save the rest of the marinade for dipping sauce.

3. Preheat the air fryer to 400°F / 204°C. Remove chicken from the marinade and place it in the air fryer. Cook for 14 minutes, turning most of the way until cooked through in the middle. Repeat for the rest of the chicken.

4. While the chicken is cooking, pour the rest of the marinade into a saucepan. Cook over medium heat until the sauce thickens and reduces down. Serve with dipping sauce and garnished with scallions.

NUTRITIONAL FACTS:
CALORIES: 297
PROTEINS: 45.5G
CARBS: 5G
FATS: 2.5G

Scallops w/ Bacon

SERVINGS: 4

INGREDIENTS:

♦ 16 lrg. scallops

♦ 8 slices bacon

♦ 16 toothpicks

♦ ¼ cup / 59ml barbeque sauce

DIRECTIONS:

1. Cut bacon slices in half and place it in the fryer at 400°F / 204°C for 3 minutes. Wipe the scallops off with paper towels. Wrap each scallop with a slice of bacon and secure it with a toothpick.

2. Spot scallops in the air fryer. Softly brush each scallop with barbeque sauce. Cook at 400°F / 204°C for 5 minutes. Turn scallops and season again with sauce. Cook for an additional 5 minutes at 400°F / 204°C until the scallop is delicate, and bacon is cooked through. Serve hot.

NUTRITIONAL FACTS:
CALORIES: 216
PROTEINS: 7G
CARBS: 1.5G
FATS: 20.5G

Chicken Parmigiana

SERVINGS: 3

INGREDIENTS:

- 3 chicken breasts
- 2 eggs
- ¼ cup / 26g breadcrumbs
- ¼ cup / 26g parmesan, grated
- ½ tsp. onion powder
- ½ tsp. Italian flavoring
- ½ tsp. garlic powder
- ½ cup / 118ml marinara sauce
- ½ cup / 113g mozzarella, shredded

DIRECTIONS:

1. In a bowl, whisk eggs, in another bowl, combine the breadcrumbs, parmesan, and onion and garlic powder.

2. Dip chicken in egg, then lay the chicken in breadcrumbs and coat liberally. Make sure to shake off the excess crumbs.

3. Spray the air fryer with non-stick cooking spray and place chicken inside.

4. Close and set the air fryer to 360°F / 182°C for 15-18 minutes or until the chicken is cooked through.

5. Open the air fryer and spoon marinara sauce over chicken and sprinkle the top with cheese. Cook for extra 2 minutes until the cheese is melted.

6. Sprinkle top with Italian seasoning and serve!

NUTRITIONAL FACTS:
CALORIES: 462
PROTEINS: 61G
CARBS: 14G
FATS: 17G

Falafel Balls

SERVINGS: 4

INGREDIENTS:

Falafel

- 1 can chickpeas, drained
- 1 cup / 227g onion, diced
- 6 cloves garlic, minced
- 1 tbsp. lemon juice, fresh
- 1 cup / 227g parsley, fresh
- ½ cup / 113g cilantro, fresh
- ¼ cup / 57g dill, fresh
- 1 tsp. baking powder
- 2 tsps. cumin
- 1 tsp. salt
- ½ cup / 113g flour
- 1 tbsp. vegetable oil

Tahini Sauce

- 1 cup yogurt
- 2 tbsps. tahini
- 2 tbsps. lemon juice, fresh

DIRECTIONS:

1. Add the chickpeas, garlic, onion, juice, cilantro, dill, parsley, cumin, baking powder, and salt into a food processor. Blitz together, stopping occasionally to scrape the sides down. Do this until the ingredients come together. Then empty the chickpea mix into a bowl and add in the four. Mix until combined thoroughly into a batter. Cover and let sit refrigerated for about 45 minutes.

2. While the falafel blend sits, you can make the tahini sauce. Combine all ingredients in a mixing bowl. Mix until combined. Cover and refrigerate until ready to use.

3. When the falafel blend is chilled, spoon a bit of the mixture into your hand and form balls. Place balls onto a baking sheet and repeat the process until the batter is all gone. Spray the air fryer bin with cooking spray. Preheat the air fryer to 375°F / 191°C.

4. Place falafel balls into the air fryer and cook for 15 minutes, remove halfway through the cooking cycle, and flip the falafel balls. Remove the falafels when done and repeat for the remaining falafel balls.

5. Serve falafel with tahini sauce for dipping. Or in a pita with lettuce, tomato onion, and the tahini sauce.

NUTRITIONAL FACTS:
CALORIES: 46
PROTEINS: 1G
CARBS: 6G
FATS: 2G

Buffalo Cauliflower Nuggets

SERVINGS: 4

INGREDIENTS:

- ◆ 1 head cauliflower
- ◆ 2 tbsps. butter
- ◆ 1 tbsp. olive oil
- ◆ ½ cup / 118ml hot sauce
- ◆ ½ cup / 113g almond flour
- ◆ 3 tbsps. dried parsley
- ◆ ½ tbsp. garlic powder
- ◆ 1 tsp. seasoning salt

DIRECTIONS:

1. Cut up the cauliflower into florets, place in a large bowl and set to the side.

2. Melt the butter and then mix olive oil and hot sauce into the butter until completely combined.

3. Pour the hot sauce blend over the cauliflower and toss until coated. In a different bowl, whisk together almond flour, parsley, garlic powder, and seasoning salt.

4. Sprinkle some of the almond flour blends over the cauliflower and toss again until coated. Move half of the cauliflower to the air fryer.

5. Air fry at 350°F / 177°C for 15 minutes, shaking multiple times during the cooking procedure. Remove cauliflower from the fryer and set it to the side. Repeat the process with the remaining cauliflower.

6. Serve with celery sticks and blue cheese dressing along with sweet potato fries.

NUTRITIONAL FACTS:
CALORIES: 204
PROTEINS: 6G
CARBS: 12G
FATS: 17G

Zesty Meatball

SERVINGS: 4

INGREDIENTS:

- 1 lb. / 454g ground beef or pork (or a mixture of both)
- ½ cup / 113g breadcrumbs
- ½ cup / 113g Parmesan, grated
- ¼ cup / 59ml milk
- 2 cloves garlic, minced
- ½ tsp. Italian flavoring
- ¾ tsp. salt
- ¼ tsp. pepper

DIRECTIONS:

1. Mix all the ingredients together in a large bowl. Then spoon out a bit of the mixture and form a ball. Repeat the process until the meat mixture is all gone.

2. Put the meatballs into the air fryer bushel in an even layer making sure that none of them are touching.

3. Air fry the meatballs at 375°F / 191°C for 15 minutes. Repeat the process for any remaining meatballs. Serve with your choice of dipping sauce, in a sandwich, in a sauce or with rice.

NUTRITIONAL FACTS:
CALORIES: 326
PROTEINS: 35G
CARBS: 6.8G
FATS: 16.8G

Empanadas con Salsa

SERVINGS: 8

INGREDIENTS:

- 8 empanada wrappers
- 1 cup / 234ml salsa
- 1 egg white
- 1 tsp. water

DIRECTIONS:

1. Preheat the air fryer to 325°F / 163°C for 8 minutes. Spray the fryer liberally with cooking spray.

2. Lay out the wrappers and place 2 tbsps of salsa in the center. Using a fork, fold the wrapper over and crimp the edges together. Repeat for the remaining empanadas.

3. Whisk the egg white with water and then brush over the tops of the sealed empanadas.

4. Fry 2 for about 8 minutes. Remove from the fryer and repeat with the remaining empanadas. Serve warm with your favorite dipping sauces.

NUTRITIONAL FACTS:
CALORIES: 183
PROTEINS: 11G
CARBS: 22G
FATS: 5G

Pot Stickers

INGREDIENTS:

- 8 oz. / 227g frozen premade dumplings

Dipping sauce

- ¼ cup / 59ml soy sauce
- ¼ cup / 59ml water
- 1/8 cup / 30ml maple syrup
- ½ tsp. garlic powder
- ½ tsp. rice vinegar
- Pinch of red pepper flakes

DIRECTIONS:

1. Preheat the air fryer to 370°F / 188°C for about 4 minutes. Place the dumplings into the air fryer and spray with cooking spray.

2. Cook for 5 minutes, shaking halfway through. Lightly respray the dumplings with cooking spray. Cook dumplings for another 4-6 minutes.

3. While cooking the dumplings make the dipping sauce. Combine all the ingredients into a bowl and whisk until combined. Remove the dumpling and let sit for a few minutes.

4. Serve warm with another Asian dish and rice

NUTRITIONAL FACTS:
CALORIES: 233
PROTEINS: 18G
CARBS: 26G
FATS: 7G

Glazed Salmon

SERVINGS: 4

INGREDIENTS:

- 4 salmon filets
- Salt and pepper to taste
- 2 tsps. soy sauce
- 1 tbsp. honey
- 1 tsp. sesame seeds

DIRECTIONS:

1. Preheat the air fryer to 375°F / 190°C. While heating the fryer, season the salmon filets with salt and pepper. Then brush the soy sauce onto the filet as well. Place in the air fryer and cook with the skin side down for 8 minutes.

2. A few minutes before salmon is done, drizzle the honey over the top and sprinkle sesame seed on them.

3. Serve with a grain of your choice or with a nice salad. (Can be served cold as well.)

NUTRITIONAL FACTS:
CALORIES: 262
PROTEINS: 34G
CARBS: 5G
FATS: 11G

Shrimp Fajitas

SERVINGS: 12

INGREDIENTS:

- 1 lb. / 454g shrimp
- 1 bell pepper, red, diced
- 1 bell pepper, green, diced
- ½ cup / 113g onion, diced
- 2 tbsps. taco seasoning
- Cooking spray
- Corn/flour tortillas

DIRECTIONS:

1. Spray the air fryer with cooking spray. Add in the shrimp, peppers, onion, and seasonings to the bin. Spray the ingredients with cooking spray and mix everything together.

2. Cook at 390°F / 199°C for 12 minutes. Open the top and spray the shrimp again with cooking spray, mixing it again when done. Cook for an extra 10 minutes.

3. Serve on warm tortillas topped with your favorite toppings.

```
NUTRITIONAL FACTS:
CALORIES: 86
PROTEINS: 10G
CARBS: 6G
FATS: 2G
```

Desserts

Churros w/ Chocolate Sauce

SERVINGS: 4

INGREDIENTS:

Churros

- 1 can refrigerated crescent rolls
- 2 tbsps. sugar
- 1 tbsp. cinnamon
- 2 tbsps. butter

Chocolate Sauce

- ½ cup / 113g dark chocolate chips
- 1 tsp. cinnamon
- 1/8 tsp. cayenne pepper
- ¼ cup / 118ml heavy cream

DIRECTIONS:

1. Preheat the air fryer to 330°F / 166°C. In a bowl, whisk together sugar and cinnamon. Unroll the dough onto a floured working surface. Cut into squares and brush melted butter over each.

2. Sprinkle two of the squares with 2 tsps. of the cinnamon-sugar. Place them on top of the other squares. Then flatten together. Using a pizza cutter, cut these squares into strips.

3. Twist each strip and then place it on the baking sheet. Repeat for remaining dough. Place in an air fryer and cook for about six minutes. Remove and repeat for remaining churros. Brush the churros with the melted butter and sprinkle the rest of the cinnamon-sugar blend over them while hot.

4. While the churros are cooking, add the chocolate, and seasonings into a mixing bowl. Then heat cream in a saucepan over low heat. When hot, add the chocolate into the cream and whisk continuously until the chips are melted. Then pour into a ramekin and serve with the warm churros.

NUTRITIONAL FACTS:
CALORIES: 128
PROTEINS: 1.4G
CARBS: 11.6G
FATS: 9G

Banana Boat S'mores

SERVINGS: 4

INGREDIENTS:

- 4 bananas
- 3 tbsps. small dark chocolate chips
- 3 tbsps. small peanut butter chips
- 3 tbsps. small marshmallows
- 3 tbsps. graham cracker crumbs

DIRECTIONS:

1. Preheat the air fryer to 400ºF / 204°C. Cut a slit in each unpeeled banana lengthwise. Open the banana up slightly.

2. Fill each pocket with chocolate chips, peanut butter chips, and marshmallows. Stick the graham cracker crumbs into the banana as well.

3. Place the bananas into the air fryer laying them on one another to keep them from falling over while cooking. Air-fry for 6 minutes.

4. Let them cool for a few minutes and serve.

NUTRITIONAL FACTS:
CALORIES: 47
PROTEINS: 4G
CARBS: 9.5G
FATS: 1.2G

Key Lime Cupcakes

SERVINGS: 6

INGREDIENTS:

- 8 oz. / 250g Greek yogurt
- 7 oz. / 200g cream cheese
- 2 lrg. eggs
- 1 lrg. egg yolk
- ¼ cup / 57g caster sugar
- 1 tsp. vanilla extract
- 2 limes, juiced and zested

DIRECTIONS:

1. Combine with a hand blender the yogurt and the cream cheese until fluffy. Then add the eggs and mix again. Now add in the sugar, vanilla extract, and the lime juice and zest. Mix again.

2. Spoon the mixture into a silicone cupcake sheet. Set the rest of the batter aside for the next batch.

3. Bake the cupcakes in the Air fryer at 320°F / 160°C for 10 minutes. Then turn the fryer up to 350°F / 180°C for a further 10 minutes.

4. When the cupcakes are done, remove and let cool. Repeat process with remaining batter.

NUTRITIONAL FACTS:
CALORIES: 218
PROTEINS: 9G
CARBS: 13G
FATS: 14G

Fried Oreos

SERVINGS: 9

INGREDIENTS:

♦ 9 Oreo cookies

♦ 1 can premade rolls

DIRECTIONS:

1. Open can of premade rolls and roll out onto a floured working surface. Cut the dough into 9 squares. Place Oreos in the center of each and wrap them with the dough.

2. Preheat air fryer to 360°F / 180°C. Place dough covered Oreos into the air fryer and cook for 4 minutes, shaking and flipping midway.

3. When done, remove from the air fryer and sprinkle with powdered sugar or cinnamon and serve!

NUTRITIONAL FACTS:
CALORIES: 67
PROTEINS: 1G
CARBS: 10G
FATS: 3G

Lava Cake

SERVINGS: 4

INGREDIENTS:

- 1½ tbsps. self-rising flour
- 3½ tbsps. caster's sugar
- 3½ oz. / 104ml butter
- 3½ oz. / 99g dark chocolate, chopped
- 2 eggs

DIRECTIONS:

1. Oil and flour 4 ramekins. Preheat the air fryer to 375°F / 190°C. Soften chocolate and butter in a microwave-safe bowl on low for 3 minutes, mixing every minute. Remove and mix until smooth.

2. Whisk the eggs and sugar in a bowl until frothy. Pour chocolate blend into egg blend slowly mixing as you do. Then add in the flour and mix. Continue mixing until smooth with no lumps.

3. Fill the ramekins around 3/4 full with cake blend and bake for 10 minutes. Remove from the fryer and let cool. Then flip the ramekin onto a plate carefully. Tap the bottom with a butter knife. Once the cake is removed, serve warm with ice cream or fruit sauce.

NUTRITIONAL FACTS:
CALORIES: 234
PROTEINS: 9.8G
CARBS: 7G
FATS: 19.2G

Beignets

INGREDIENTS:

- ◆ Cooking spray
- ◆ ½ cup / 113g all-purpose flour
- ◆ ¼ cup / 57g white sugar
- ◆ ⅛ cup / 19ml water
- ◆ 1 lrg. egg
- ◆ 1½ tsp. butter
- ◆ ½ tsp. baking powder
- ◆ ½ tsp. vanilla extract
- ◆ Pinch of salt
- ◆ 2 tbsps. powdered sugar

DIRECTIONS:

1. Preheat the air fryer to 370°F / 185°C. Lightly coat a silicone baking dish with cooking spray.

2. Whisk flour, sugar, water, egg yolk, butter, baking powder, vanilla extract, and salt together in a bowl until combined thoroughly.

3. Beat the egg white in a separate bowl using a hand mixer on medium speed until peaks begin to form. Then fold egg whites into the batter carefully. Add batter to a silicone baking dish with an ice cream scoop.

4. Place a silicone dish into the air fryer and bake for 10 minutes. Remove silicone dish and flip the beignets. Place back in the fryer and bake for an additional 4 minutes.

5. Remove beignets from the air fryer and garnish with confectioners' sugar.

NUTRITIONAL FACTS:
CALORIES: 88
PROTEINS: 2G
CARBS: 16.2G
FATS: 1.7G

Banana Cake

SERVINGS: 4

INGREDIENTS:

- ♦ Cooking spray
- ♦ ⅓ cup / 85g brown sugar
- ♦ 3½ tbsps. butter
- ♦ 1 banana, mashed
- ♦ 1 egg
- ♦ 2 tbsps. honey
- ♦ 1 cup / 227g self-rising flour
- ♦ ½ tsp. ground cinnamon
- ♦ Pinch of salt

DIRECTIONS:

1. Preheat an air fryer to 320°F / 160°C. Lightly coat a small Bundt cake pan with cooking spray.

2. Beat sugar and butter together in a bowl with an electric blender until smooth. Then add banana, egg, and honey in a different bowl mixing until combined. Now add the butter mixture to the banana and whisk to combine.

3. Sift the flour, cinnamon, and salt into the batter blend. Blend until smooth. Pour into the Bundt cake pan and place it in the air fryer. Move to the readied container; level the surface utilizing the rear of a spoon.

4. Cook for 30 minutes or until a toothpick can be removed clean. Serve with warm chocolate sauce or dusted with powdered sugar.

NUTRITIONAL FACTS:
CALORIES: 347
PROTEINS: 5.2G
CARBS: 57G
FATS: 11.8G

Snacks

Sweet Potato Chips

SERVINGS: 6

INGREDIENTS:

- 2 med. sweet potatoes, sliced
- ¼ cup / 118ml olive oil
- 1 tsp. ground cinnamon
- Salt and pepper to taste

DIRECTIONS:

1. Cut the sweet potatoes into rounds with a mandolin. Submerge chips in cold water for 30 minutes. Drain and let chips dry completely.

2. In a bowl, combine the oil and seasonings and then toss the chips in the mix until coated. Lightly coat the air fryer with cooking spray.

3. In batches, cook the sweet potato chips at 390°F / 199°C for 20 minutes, giving the container a shake each 7 to 8 minutes. Remove and adjust seasoning if needed. Serve hot with ketchup.

NUTRITIONAL FACTS:
CALORIES: 122
PROTEINS: 1G
CARBS: 10G
FATS: 9.1G

Hard-Boiled Eggs

SERVINGS: 6

INGREDIENTS:

♦ 6 lrg. eggs

DIRECTIONS:

1. Set your wire rack inside the air fryer and place the eggs on top of the wire rack.

2. Cook at 250°F / 121°C for about 16 minutes. After the eggs, take them out and put them in an ice bath to stop the cooking. Peel and eat!

> **NUTRITIONAL FACTS:**
> CALORIES: 77
> PROTEINS: 6.3G
> CARBS: .6G
> FATS: 5G

Kale Chips

SERVINGS: 2

INGREDIENTS:

- 2 tbsps. olive oil
- 4 cups / 907g kale
- 2 tsps. ranch dressing seasoning
- 1 tbsp. nutritional yeast
- ¼ tsp. salt

DIRECTIONS:

1. Toss the oil, kale, seasoning, and yeast together in a bowl. Mix until the kale is coated with the mixture and then dump onto the air fryer sheet.

2. Cook on 370°F / 188°C for 4-5 minutes, shaking after 2 minutes. Remove from the air fryer and enjoy it.

NUTRITIONAL FACTS:
CALORIES: 161
PROTEINS: 3.7G
CARBS: 6.3G
FATS: 13.9G

Apple Chips

SERVINGS: 4

INGREDIENTS:

- 6 lrg. apples
- 1 tsp. olive oil
- Pinch of cinnamon

DIRECTIONS:

1. Slice up your apple into thin slices with a mandolin. Place them in the air fryer and sprinkle with a teaspoon of olive oil.

2. Cook at 356°F / 180°C for 10 minutes or until nicely browned. Then remove the chips and toss them with cinnamon. Serve!

NUTRITIONAL FACTS:
CALORIES: 231
PROTEINS: 1.1G
CARBS: 55G
FATS: 1G

Seasoned Chickpeas

SERVINGS: 8

INGREDIENTS:

- 1 can chickpeas
- 1 tbsp. olive oil
- 4 tsps. dried dill
- 2 tsps. garlic powder
- 2 tsps. onion powder
- ¾ tsp. salt
- 1 tbsp. lemon juice, fresh

DIRECTIONS:

1. In a bowl, add the chickpeas and 1 tablespoon of their fluid from the can. Air fry at 400° F / 204°C for 12 minutes.

2. Remove chickpeas and put them in a bowl. Add the olive oil, dill, garlic powder, onion powder, salt, and lemon juice. Toss the chickpeas until they are completely covered.

3. Place the chickpeas back into the air fryer and cook at 350°F / 177°C for 5 more minutes

4. Serve warm or let chill and store for a snack later.

NUTRITIONAL FACTS:
CALORIES: 119
PROTEINS: 5.4G
CARBS: 17.7G
FATS: 3.5G

Bonus: 14 Day Meal Plan

DAY 1

Breakfast – Breakfast Hand Pies

SERVINGS: 4

INGREDIENTS:

- ◆ 1 package puff pastry sheets
- ◆ 5 eggs
- ◆ ½ cup / 227g maple flavored breakfast sausage
- ◆ ½ cup/ 227g bacon
- ◆ ½ cup / 227g cheddar, shredded

DIRECTIONS:

1. Heat butter in a skillet and scramble the eggs. Then add sausage and bacon into eggs and cook.

2. Roll out puff pastry on a floured working surface. Cut into squares. Then spoon a little of the mixture into the center of half of the squares. Place one square on each of the filled squares and using a fork crimp the edges together

3. Lightly spray the squares with cooking spray and place them in the air fryer. Bake for 8-10 minutes at 370°F / 188°C.

4. Bake until browned and repeat if needed. Serve warm or freeze to be heated later.

> **NUTRITIONAL FACTS:**
> CALORIES: 218
> PROTEINS: 13.1G
> CARBS: 2.4G
> FATS: 17.4G

Lunch – Avocado fries w/ Bacon (See page 34)

Dinner – Asian Glazed Chicken (See page 48)

DAY 2

Breakfast – Walnut & Cinnamon Baked Apples (See page 20)

Lunch – Vegan Tacos

SERVINGS: 4

INGREDIENTS:

- ◆ 4 cups / 907g cauliflower
- ◆ 1 can chickpeas, drained and rinsed

- ◆ 2 tbsps. olive oil
- ◆ 2 tbsps. taco seasoning

To serve

- ◆ 8 tortillas
- ◆ 2 avocados. diced
- ◆ 4 cups / 907g cabbage, shredded
- ◆ coconut yogurt

DIRECTIONS:

1. Preheat air fryer to 390°F / 200°C. In a bowl, combine the cauliflower and chickpeas with the olive oil and taco seasoning. Dump everything into the air fryer.

2. Cook for 20 minutes, or until cauliflower is cooked and lightly browned.

3. Serve in tortillas topped with avocado, cabbage, and coconut yogurt.

NUTRITIONAL FACTS:
CALORIES: 508
PROTEINS: 20G
CARBS: 77G
FATS: 15G

Dinner – Scallops w/ Bacon (See page 50)

DAY 3

Breakfast – Cheesy Sausage & Pepper Breakfast Casserole (See page 21)

Lunch – Antipasto Pockets (See page 35)

Dinner – Eggplant Parmesan

SERVINGS: 4

INGREDIENTS:

- 1 lrg. eggplant
- ½ cup / 53g whole-wheat breadcrumbs
- 3 tbsps. parmesan, grated
- salt to taste
- 1 tsp. Italian seasoning
- 3 tbsps. entire wheat flour
- 1 egg
- 1 tbsp water
- Cooking spray
- 1 cup / 237ml marinara sauce
- ¼ cup / 57g mozzarella, shredded
- Basil, fresh, chopped

DIRECTIONS:

1. Cut eggplant into about slices. Rub salt on each side and leave it for about 10-15 mins. While the eggplant sets, mix the egg and water together in a bowl and put flour in another bowl. On a separate plate, mix the breadcrumbs, parmesan, and seasoning. Add to the egg and water mixture.

2. Dip the eggplant in the flour, then the egg and finally into the breadcrumb mix. Place the breaded eggplant on a baking sheet. Preheat the air fryer to 360°F / 182°C.

3. Then spray the eggplant with cooking spray and place it in the air fryer. Cook for 8 minutes, flipping the eggplant halfway through. Then add some marinara and top with cheese and cook for another couple of minutes.

4. Serve warm on your preferred pasta.

NUTRITIONAL FACTS:
CALORIES: 100
PROTEINS: 6.4G
CARBS: 17.7G
FATS: 1.5G

DAY 4

Breakfast – Egg in a Basket

Servings: 1

INGREDIENTS:

- 1 slice of bread
- 1 egg
- salt and pepper to taste

DIRECTIONS:

1. Spray your air fryer with non-stick cooking spray and place your slice of bread into the air fryer. Then scoop out the center and crack an egg inside of that hole.

2. Cook at 330°F / 166°C for 6 minutes, at that point, utilize a spatula and flip the egg, and cook for another 3-4 minutes.

> NUTRITIONAL FACTS:
> CALORIES: 274
> PROTEINS: 14G
> CARBS: 24.4G
> FATS: 13.4G

Lunch – Chicken Stuffed Quesadilla (See page 36)

Dinner – Glazed Salmon (See page 60)

DAY 5

Breakfast – Cinnamon Rolls (See page 22)

Lunch – Taquitos

Servings: 6

INGREDIENTS:

Taquitos

- Cooking spray
- 3 cups / 680g chicken, cooked, shredded
- 1 package cream cheese
- 1 chipotle pepper in adobo sauce, chopped (with 1 tbsp. sauce reserved)
- 1 tsp. cumin
- 1 tsp. chili powder
- Salt and pepper to taste
- 12 corn tortillas
- ½ cup / 113g cheddar, shredded
- ½ cup / 113g pepper jack, shredded
- Salsa

Avocado Cream Sauce

- 1 lrg. avocado, diced
- ½ cup / 118ml sour cream
- ¼ cup cilantro, fresh
- 1 clove garlic
- 1 lime, juiced
- Salt and pepper to taste

DIRECTIONS:

1. In a bowl, mix the chicken, cream cheese, chipotle and sauce, cumin, and chili powder together. Season with salt and pepper.

2. Place tortillas on a microwave-safe plate and cover with a soggy paper towel. Microwave 30 seconds, or until warm and more malleable.

3. Spread about some of the fillings on one side of the tortilla. Then sprinkle some cheese and roll. Repeat until all the taquitos are made.

4. Place in the air fryer, crease side down, and cook at 400°F / 204°C for 7 minutes.

5. While the taquitos are cooking, combine all the ingredients for the sauce in a food processor. Pulse until smooth and combined. Then when taquitos are done, serve hot with dipping sauce and salsa.

NUTRITIONAL FACTS:
CALORIES: 598
PROTEINS: 24G
CARBS: 9G
FATS: 52.5G

Dinner – Zesty Meatball (See page 57)

DAY 6

Breakfast – Sugared Doughnuts (See page 24)

Lunch – Cauliflower Bits (See page 37)

Dinner – Sesame Chicken

Servings: 6

INGREDIENTS:

Chicken

- 6 chicken thighs, boneless, skinless
- ½ cup / 113g cornstarch
- Cooking spray

Sauce

- ¼ cup / 59ml soy sauce
- 2 tbsps. brown sugar
- 2 tbsps. orange juice, fresh
- 5 tsps. Hoisin sauce
- ½ tsp. ground ginger
- 1 clove garlic, minced
- 1 tbsp. water
- 1 tbsp. Cornstarch
- 2 tsps. sesame seeds

DIRECTIONS:

1. Cut the chicken into cubes and toss with cornstarch. Place in the air fryer and cook at 390°F / 199°C for 24 minutes, flipping the check halfway through the cooking process.

2. While the chicken is cooking, in a saucepan, start the sauce. Combine the soy sauce, orange juice, brown sugar, ground ginger, hoisin sauce, and garlic to the pan and cook over medium. Stir to combine.

3. Mix the cornstarch and water together to create a slurry. When the sugar has completely melted and the mixture is simmering, add the slurry. Blend in the sesame seeds.

4. Remove the sauce from the heat and set to the side. Then when the chicken is done, place in a bowl and coat it with the sauce.

5. Serve bested over rice and beans.

NUTRITIONAL FACTS:
CALORIES: 335
PROTEINS: 30G
CARBS: 28G
FATS: 12G

DAY 7

Breakfast – Denver Omelet

SERVINGS: 4

INGREDIENTS:

- ♦ 2 eggs
- ♦ ¼ cup / 59ml milk
- ♦ Pinch of salt
- ♦ Ham, peppers, and onions chopped
- ♦ 1 tsp. seasoning blend of choice
- ♦ ¼ cup / 57g cheddar, shredded

DIRECTIONS:

1. In a bowl, blend the eggs and milk until combined. Add a touch of salt to the egg blend. Then include the veggies and meat into the egg mixture.

2. Pour the egg mixture into an oiled dish and place it in the air fryer. Cook at 350ºF / 177°C for 8-10 minutes. Halfway through cooking, sprinkle the top withs seasoning and additional cheese.

3. When done, use a spatula or butter knife to release the omelet onto a plate. Serve warm garnished with scallions.

> **NUTRITIONAL FACTS:**
> CALORIES: 107
> PROTEINS: 7G
> CARBS: 1.7G
> FATS: 7.8G

Lunch – Crispy Chicken Fingers (See page 39)

Dinner – Shrimp Fajitas (See page 61)

DAY 8

Breakfast – Avocado Cups (See page 26)

Lunch – Crispy Pickle Slices

SERVINGS: 3

INGREDIENTS:

- 2 cups / 454g dill pickle chips
- 1 egg
- 1 tbsp. water
- ½ cup / 53g breadcrumbs
- ¼ cup / 57g Parmesan, grated
- 1 tsp. dried oregano
- 1 tsp. garlic powder
- Ranch dressing

DIRECTIONS:

1. Pat pickle chips dry with paper towels. In a bowl, mix together breadcrumbs, parmesan, oregano, and garlic powder. Mix the egg with water and whisk together.

2. Dip pickle chips first in the egg mixture and afterward in the breadcrumb blend. Working in batches, place pickles in a single layer in the air fryer bin. Cook at 400°F / 204°C for 10 minutes.

3. Serve warm with ranch.

NUTRITIONAL FACTS:
CALORIES: 107
PROTEINS: 7.6G
CARBS: 7.3G
FATS: 5.2G

Dinner – Chicken Parmesan (See page 51)

DAY 9

Breakfast – French Toast Sticks (See page 27)

Lunch – Thai-Styled Salmon Cakes (See page 41)

Dinner – Fried Fish

SERVINGS: 8

INGREDIENTS:

- 8 fish filets
- 1 tbsp. olive oil
- 1 cup / 107g breadcrumbs
- ½ tsp. paprika
- ¼ tsp. chili powder
- ¼ tsp. pepper
- ¼ tsp. garlic powder
- ¼ tsp. onion powder
- ½ tsp. salt

DIRECTIONS:

1. Spray with cooking spray. In a shallow dish, mix the breadcrumbs with paprika, chili powder, pepper, garlic powder, onion powder, and salt. Coat each fish filet in breadcrumbs and place them in the air fryer.

2. Cook at 390°F / 200°C for 12-15 minutes. After 8-10 minutes, flip the fish fillets and keep cooking.

3. Serve with fries or steamed veggies.

NUTRITIONAL FACTS:
CALORIES: 153
PROTEINS: 21G
CARBS: 11G
FATS: 3G

DAY 10

Breakfast – Biscuit Bombs

Servings: 8

INGREDIENTS:

Roll Bombs

- 4 slices bacon
- 1 tbsp. butter
- 2 eggs
- ¼ tsp. pepper
- 1 can rolls
- 2 oz. / 57g sharp cheddar, cubed

Egg Wash

- 1 egg
- 1 tbsp. water

DIRECTIONS:

1. Cut two circles of parchment paper. Place one in the base of the air fryer and spray with cooking spray.

2. In a skillet, cook bacon over medium-high until crispy. Remove from the skillet and set on a paper towel. Wipe the skillet out and add butter. When melted, pour in the eggs and scramble the season to taste as you go. Remove and stir in the bacon. Let stand for a few minutes.

3. In the meantime, separate the rolls into portions and split those two in half. Place a spoonful of the mixture into each biscuit half, top with cheese, and cover with the other part. Press the edges to seal. Mix egg and water together and brush the egg wash on all sides of the biscuit.

4. Place biscuits into the air fryer and cook at 325°F / 163°C to cook for 8 minutes.

NUTRITIONAL FACTS:
CALORIES: 200
PROTEINS: 7G
CARBS: 17G
FATS: 12G

Lunch – Tofu Bites (See page 43)

Dinner – Empanada con Salsa (See page 58)

DAY 11

Breakfast – Keto-Styled Baked Eggs (See page 28)

Lunch – Classic Chicken Wings

SERVINGS: 4

INGREDIENTS:

- ½ lb. chicken wings
- 1 tbsp. olive oil
- ¼ tsp. pepper
- ½ tsp. salt

DIRECTIONS:

1. Preheat the air fryer to 390°F / 200°C. Pat the chicken wings dry with a paper towel. Then in a bowl, combine the olive oil, salt, and pepper. Toss in the chicken wings and coat with mixture.

2. Place the wings in the air fryer and cook for 25-35 minutes, shaking at regular intervals.

3. Cook until crispy and brown. Serve with the dipping sauce of your choice and fries.

NUTRITIONAL FACTS:
CALORIES: 235
PROTEINS: 16G
CARBS: 0G
FATS: 18G

Dinner – Buffalo Cauliflower Nuggets (See page 55)

DAY 12

Breakfast – Vegetable Quiche (See page 29)

Lunch – Crunchy Cheese Sticks (See page 44)

Dinner – Pork Tenderloin

SERVINGS: 4

INGREDIENTS:

- ¼ cup / 59ml Dijon mustard
- 2 tbsps. brown sugar
- 1 tsp. dried parsley
- ½ tsp. dried thyme
- ¼ tsp. salt
- ¼ tsp. pepper
- 1¼ lb. / 567g pork tenderloin
- ¾ lb. / 340g baby potatoes
- 1 bundle green beans, cut
- 1 tbsp. olive oil
- Salt and pepper to taste

DIRECTIONS:

1. Preheat an air fryer to 400°F / 200°C. Whisk mustard, brown sugar, parsley, thyme, salt, and pepper together in a bowl. Place tenderloin into the bowl and coat with mustard mixture.

2. Add the potatoes, green beans, and olive oil into a different bowl. Season with salt and pepper to taste and toss until coated. Set to the side.

3. Set the tenderloin in the pre-heated air fryer and cook, undisturbed, for about 20 minutes. Move to a cutting board and let rest for 10 minutes.

4. Then, place green beans and potatoes into the air fryer and cook for 10 minutes, shaking part of the way through cook time.

5. Cut tenderloin and serve with potatoes and green beans.

NUTRITIONAL FACTS:
CALORIES: 286
PROTEINS: 25.4G
CARBS: 31.4G
FATS: 6.5G

DAY 13

Breakfast – Pumpkin Muffins

SERVINGS: 12

INGREDIENTS:

- 1 cup / 237ml pumpkin puree
- 2 cups / 454g oats
- ½ cup / 118ml honey
- 2 eggs
- 1 tsps. coconut butter
- 1 tbsp. cocoa nibs
- 1 tbsp. vanilla extract
- 1 tsp. nutmeg

DIRECTIONS:

1. Combine ingredients into a blender and mix until smooth. Spoon mixture into a silicone muffin dish.

2. Place in the fryer and cook for 15 minutes at 356°F / 180°C. When done, remove and let cool on a rack.

NUTRITIONAL FACTS:
CALORIES: 121
PROTEINS: 3G
CARBS: 22G
FATS: 2G

Lunch – Pizza Margherita (See page 45)

Dinner – Falafel Balls (See page 53)

DAY 14

Breakfast – Chorizo & Egg Burrito (See page 30)

Lunch – Crispy Tortellini

SERVINGS: 6

INGREDIENTS:

- 1 package cheese tortellini
- 1 cup / 107g breadcrumbs
- 1/3 cup / 85g Parmesan, grated
- 1 tsp. dried oregano
- ½ tsp. garlic powder
- ½ tsp. red pepper flakes
- Salt and pepper to taste
- 1 cup / 227g all-purpose flour
- 2 lrg. eggs
- Marinara

DIRECTIONS:

1. Cook tortellini according to instructions and then drain.

2. In a bowl, combine breadcrumbs, garlic powder, oregano, parmesan, and red pepper flakes. Season with salt and pepper. Then beat the eggs in a separate bowl, and in a third bowl, add the flour.

3. Coat tortellini in flour, then the egg mix, and finally the breadcrumbs.

4. Place in the air fryer and fry at 370°F / 188°C until lightly browned, 10 minutes.

5. Serve with marinara and a salad.

> **NUTRITIONAL FACTS:**
> CALORIES: 130
> PROTEINS: 5G
> CARBS: 22.7G
> FATS: 2G

Dinner – Pot Stickers (See page 59)

EXCLUSIVE BONUS

40 Weight Loss Recipes

&

14 Days Meal Plan

Scan the QR-Code and receive
the FREE download:

Disclaimer

This book contains opinions and ideas of the author and is meant to teach the reader informative and helpful knowledge while due care should be taken by the user in the application of the information provided. The instructions and strategies are possibly not right for every reader and there is no guarantee that they work for everyone. Using this book and implementing the information/ recipes therein contained is explicitly your own responsibility and risk. This work with all its contents, does not guarantee correctness, completion, quality or correctness of the provided information. Misinformation or misprints cannot be completely eliminated.

Printed in Great Britain
by Amazon

87185463R00064